Keeping Christ's Sacred Promise

Keeping Christ's
SACRED
PROMISE

A Pastoral Framework for
INDIGENOUS MINISTRY

UNITED STATES CONFERENCE OF CATHOLIC BISHOPS

The document *Keeping Christ's Sacred Promise: A Pastoral Framework for Indigenous Ministry* was developed by the Committee on Cultural Diversity in the Church/Subcommittee on Native American Affairs of the United States Conference of Catholic Bishops (USCCB). It was approved by the full body of the USCCB at its June 2024 Plenary Assembly and has been authorized for publication by the undersigned.

Rev. Michael J.K. Fuller, S.T.D.

General Secretary, USCCB

Quotations from papal and other Vatican-generated documents including Vatican II Documents are available on vatican.va are copyright © Libreria Editrice Vaticana.

Excerpts from the Code of Canon Law: Latin-English Edition, New English Translation copyright 1998, Canon Law Society of America, Washington, DC, are reprinted with permission.

Scripture texts in this work are taken from the *New American Bible*, revised edition © 2010, 1991, 1986, 1970 Confraternity of Christian Doctrine, Washington, D.C. and are used by permission of the copyright owner. All Rights Reserved. No part of the *New American Bible* may be reproduced in any form without permission in writing from the copyright owner.

Printed in 2024 by OSV, Our Sunday Visitor, 200 Noll PLaza, Huntington, IN 46750; 1-800-348-2440; www.osv.com.

ISBN: 978-1-63966-327-9 (Inventory No. T2970)
eISBN: 978-1-63966-328-6

Cover art: *Indigenous Christ* by Charles Rencountre. Copyright © Sioux Spiritual Center, Diocese of Rapid City, South Dakota. Used with permission.
Interior art: AdobeStock
Cover and interior design: Amanda Falk

PRINTED IN THE UNITED STATES OF AMERICA

Table of Contents

Preface

Dear Friends in Christ,

We have developed this Pastoral Framework because as shepherds we have a sacred duty to ensure that Christ's promise is fulfilled in Catholic Indigenous communities. This framework develops a path forward in this vital ministry.

The bishops formally addressed Catholic Native Peoples in 1977 with the *Statement of U.S. Catholic Bishops on American Indians*. Since then, Catholic Native ministries and populations have experienced fundamental changes. In dialogue with Indigenous Catholic leaders, the Subcommittee on Native American Affairs of the United States Conference of Catholic Bishops (USCCB) has discerned the need for a new pastoral framework to address current realities and pastoral challenges. In consultation with the Standing Committee on Cultural Diversity in the Church, the subcommittee subsequently requested and obtained authorization from the USCCB General Assembly to draft a new pastoral framework for Native ministry to come from the full body of bishops.

In serving Native communities in their respective dioceses, bishops often come to realize the importance of listening to the Elders and other Catholic Native leaders and recognizing the wisdom of the Holy Spirit speaking through them. These leaders, through example, have taught bishops and priests, and other ministers serving among them, the importance of both listening and patience. In keeping with this synodal spirit, on March 26–27, 2019, a listening session for bishops and Native leaders was held in Phoenix. From this session was born a renewed commitment to listen more deeply, to reflect, and to put into motion the actions and recommendations emerging from these dialogues.

The Spirit of God is active, alive, and present in Native American, Alaska Native, and Native Hawaiian communities. The Subcommittee on Native American Affairs is pleased to present this Pastoral Framework to offer guidance to bishops, pastors, religious, Catholic Native leaders, and others serving Indigenous communities. Native Indigenous Peoples do not just play an essential part of the Church's history in the Americas — they are a vital part of our present. Much of what these pages offer is the product of dialogues with Native Peoples and of our collective discernment regarding their pastoral needs and the actions needed to address them.

While unable to include the voice of every single tribe, as bishops, we want to express our appreciation for those Catholic Native leaders from various parts of the country who participated in the various forms of consultation. Heeding their advice, the contents of this framework are not meant as a comprehensive treatise of "all things Native American." The purpose of this document is to lift the major topics and concerns that emerged from those conversations, and to encourage local bishops to engage and deepen the dialogue with the local Native communities.

This document is written not just for the benefit of Catholic Native communities but for the benefit of the entire Church in the United States. When the Church works with diverse cultural communities, the Church lives out being *one* and *catholic* at the same time, and it is better able to realize its mystical union with Christ. Therefore, the steps laid out in this Pastoral Framework seek to promote reconciliation and healing, proclaim the Good News of Jesus Christ, celebrate God's love for Indigenous Peoples and peoples of all cultures, and proclaim our unity in faith in the love of Christ.

Most Reverend Chad W. Zielinski
Bishop of New Ulm
Chairman, Subcommittee on Native American Affairs

Most Rev. Arturo Cepeda
Auxiliary Bishop of Detroit
Chairman, Committee on Cultural Diversity in the Church

The Gospel of Jesus Christ is at home in every people. It enriches, uplifts and purifies every culture. All of us together make up the People of God, the Body of Christ, the Church. We should all be grateful for the growing unity, presence, voice and leadership of Catholic Native Americans in the Church today.

— *Saint John Paul II**

* *Address to the Native Peoples of the Americas, Phoenix, 1987,* https://www.vatican.va/content/john-paul-ii/en /speeches/1987/september/documents/hf_jp-ii_spe_19870914_amerindi-phoenix.html

Introduction

"For the promise is made to you and to your children
and to all those far off, whomever the Lord our
God will call." — Acts of the Apostles 2:39

A s Catholic bishops, it is our sacred duty to make sure that Christ's sacred promise is kept to all his brothers and sisters. Despite a history of broken promises and failures to Indigenous populations* in the United States our God remains ever faithful. Encouraged by the promise of his Holy Spirit, which enlivens his Church, we labor to bring the Good News of salvation to all peoples. It is our duty as shepherds to promote and defend the dignity of human life, to strengthen families and communities in their faith, and to ensure they develop a strong relationship with the Lord Jesus. This Pastoral Framework is intended to help the Church in the United States keep Christ's sacred promise to his Indigenous brothers and sisters, to remind them and ourselves of God's unending love for all his children, and to enliven hope for future generations.

---

* As of the 2020 Census, the U.S. federal government uses the following official terms to identify different Indigenous groups: American Indian, Alaska Native, Native Hawaiian, and Pacific Islander. For consistency, this document prefers to apply the term "Indigenous" to Native or aboriginal peoples in general, not to particular groups. U.S. Indigenous Catholic leaders also expressed a preference for the term "Indigenous" during a listening session with Catholic bishops in 2019. This usage is also consistent with Vatican terminology. The term "Native" (for example, "Native American," "Native Peoples," "Native youth," "Native Catholics") is also acceptable and is commonly used to refer to these populations. For the purposes of this document, the terms "Indigenous" and "Native" are interchangeable, reflecting that people might prefer one or the other. See Black and Indian Mission Office and the USCCB Subcommittee on Native American Affairs, *Listening Session: March 26–27, 2019, Phoenix* (accessed April 17, 2023), *blackandindianmission.org/sites/default/files/inline-files/2019-LISTENING-SESSION.pdf*. Other Native governance resources consulted also indicate the capitalization of terms such as Native, Indigenous Peoples, Indian, and Tribe, when used both as nouns and adjectives or qualifiers.

The journey of Indigenous Catholics in the United States of America has been marked by moments of great joy but also of profound sorrow. Through this Pastoral Framework, we, the Catholic bishops of the United States, hope to begin anew a journey of mutual accompaniment with the Catholic Indigenous Peoples of these lands. We recognize that the Indigenous Peoples were the first to embrace the Catholic faith in this continent. Dedicated missionaries like St. John de Brébeuf, S.J., and St. Isaac Jogues, S.J.; St. Junípero Serra, O.F.M.; Venerable Frederic Baraga, Bishop of Marquette;* and Venerable Eusebio Francesco Chini (called "Padre Kino"), S.J., gave up their homeland, family, and everything they knew in order to spread faith in Jesus Christ to Indigenous Peoples. Through the grace of the Holy Spirit, these initial missionary efforts took root, and many embraced the Christian faith. St. Kateri Tekakwitha, the Servants of God Antonio Inija and Companions (known as the Martyrs of La Florida Missions), the Servant of God Nicholas Black Elk, and countless other Indigenous Catholics are the fruit of their ministry. These holy Indigenous men and women became witnesses to their peoples, as well as models of faith.

Today, many North American Indigenous Catholics trace their faith to the decision of their ancestors to embrace Catholicism hundreds of years ago. Sadly, many Indigenous Catholics have felt a sense of abandonment in their relationship with Church leaders due to a lack of understanding of their unique cultural needs. We apologize for the failure to nurture, strengthen, honor, recognize, and appreciate those entrusted to our pastoral care.

In July 2022, Pope Francis greeted the Inuit People in Iqaluit, the capital city of Nunavut, during his pastoral visit to Canada. In what he called a "penitential pilgrimage," he said, "We are here with the desire to pursue together a journey of healing and reconciliation that, with the help of the Creator, can help us shed light on what happened and move

---

* Venerable Frederic Baraga, Bishop of Marquette, was a missionary to the Indigenous Peoples, traveling for miles on snowshoes and in harsh conditions for the spiritual and temporal welfare of the people. He authored twenty books in the Ojibwe language, including catechisms, prayer books, and the dictionary and grammar of the language that is still being used today. As the founding bishop of the Diocese of Marquette, he issued his first pastoral letter in both English and Ojibwe. He also successfully fought against the relocation of the Indigenous Peoples. https://www.fatherbaraga.org/

beyond the dark past."†

We resolve now to prioritize our pastoral ministry with Indigenous Catholics. We seek to accompany the Indigenous Peoples of this land in their faith through praying, listening, and seeking healing and reconciliation along the way, so that we can journey together toward the house of the heavenly Father. We affirm that this accompaniment should be intentional and mutual in identifying, forming, promoting, and developing Indigenous Catholic leadership — ordained and lay — in our communities, so that they are prepared to serve as missionary disciples and as leaders in the Catholic community. Finally, we hope that this Pastoral Framework will help local churches and the wider Catholic community in the United States to receive and appreciate the gifts that Catholic Indigenous Peoples offer the Church and to be more attentive to their pastoral needs and concerns. May this document serve as the renewed welcome for Indigenous Catholics in the life of the Church.

---

† Pope Francis, Address, Meeting with Young People and Elders at a Primary School in Iqaluit, July 29, 2022, *www.vatican.va/content/francesco/en/speeches/2022/july/documents/20220729-giovani-anziani-iqaluit.html.*

PART ONE:

A Call for Healing

A HISTORY OF TRAUMA

The history of Indigenous Peoples in the United States of America is punctuated by trauma. Before the arrival of Europeans in the late-fifteenth and sixteenth centuries, the American continent was inhabited by Indigenous People. For millennia, this was their home.[*] Among the most significant sources of trauma are epidemics, national policies, and Native boarding schools, which stand out because of their profound effect on family life. The family systems of many Indigenous Peoples never fully recovered from these tragedies, which often led to broken homes harmed by addiction, domestic abuse, abandonment, and neglect. The Church recognizes that it has played a part in traumas experienced by Native children.

People from Europe and Asia unknowingly brought with them viruses and bacteria to which Indigenous communities had no natural or acquired immunity. Many Indigenous communities were brought to the brink of extinction, and in some cases were actually made extinct, by the ensuing epidemics. We may never know the extent of the loss of population, but historians estimate that epidemics claimed the lives of nearly 80 to 90 percent of the Indigenous population throughout the Americas, especially in the first 150 years after the arrival of Christopher Columbus to the Americas.[†] In some regions, entire families and villages were wiped out. Those who remained often had to pick up the pieces of their way of life without intact family and tribal systems to rely on. Missionaries who shared the Gospel of Jesus Christ sought to support the Indigenous communities amid this devastating trauma.

The government of the newly founded United States of America established initiatives detrimental to the Indigenous families; some of

---

[*] During the Colonial Period the conquest and occupation of North America by the great European powers — England, Spain, France, and the Netherlands — devastated and defrauded the Native population through disease, warfare, land dispossession, trader fraud, relocation, and murder. See Scott Weidensaul, *The First Frontier*, Houghton Mifflin Harcourt, 2012.

[†] See Nathan Nunn and Nancy Qian, "The Columbian Exchange: A History of Disease, Food, and Ideas," *Journal of Economic Perspectives* 24, no. 2 (Spring 2010): 163–188, *doi.org/10.1257/jep.24.2.163.*

these policies forced many Indigenous Peoples to relocate to reservations. Sadly, these actions exterminated many Indigenous communities. In other communities, forced relocation disrupted an established way of life. For cultures based on fishing, land cultivation, and hunting, this new way of life — dependent on government subsidies for food and other resources — resulted in losses of meaning and purpose. These profound changes often contributed to depression, addiction, and further breakdowns of the family unit.

Regrettably, European and Eurocentric world powers — exploiting language from fourteenth- and fifteenth-century papal letters known as "bulls" — developed their own justifications to enslave, mistreat, and remove Indigenous Peoples from their lands. These ideologies — that is, the legal and political systems and related practices that developed from them — are collectively known as the "doctrine of discovery."

Let us be very clear here: The Catholic Church does not espouse these ideologies. The Vatican Dicasteries for Culture and Education and for Promoting Integral Human Development emphasize that the "Church's magisterium" upholds the respect due to every human being. The Catholic Church therefore repudiates those concepts that fail to recognize the inherent human rights of Indigenous peoples, including what has become known as the legal and political "doctrine of discovery." In a joint 2023 statement, the dicasteries clearly state:

> The "doctrine of discovery" is not part of the teaching of the Catholic Church. Historical research clearly demonstrates that the papal documents in question, written in a specific historical period and linked to political questions, have never been considered expressions of the Catholic faith. At the same time, the Church acknowledges that these papal bulls did not adequately reflect the equal dignity and rights of indigenous peoples. The Church is also aware that the contents of these documents were manipulated for political purposes by competing colonial powers in order to justify immoral acts against indigenous peoples that were carried out, at times, without opposition from ecclesiastical authorities. It is only just to recognize these errors, ac-

knowledge the terrible effects of the assimilation policies and the pain experienced by indigenous peoples, and ask for pardon. Furthermore, Pope Francis has urged: "Never again can the Christian community allow itself to be infected by the idea that one culture is superior to others, or that it is legitimate to employ ways of coercing others."*

The experiences and histories of different countries and different Indigenous peoples are distinct, but in the broader discussion of the "doctrine of discovery" lies a unique opportunity for constructive dialogue and a collaborative pathway to discuss important issues concerning Native Americans, Alaska Natives, and Native Hawaiians. This collaboration represents an important way to find a peaceful path forward, especially when we address different historical methods of forced assimilation.

In the United States, forced removals to reservations were followed by policies of cultural assimilation, in which the government of the United States attempted to force Tribes to conform to the dominant American culture. Through its Bureau of Indian Affairs, the government established more than four hundred boarding schools[†] across the United States and forced many Indigenous children to attend them. In these schools, Indigenous children were forced to abandon their traditional languages, dress, and customs.

Boarding schools were seen as one expedient means to achieve this cultural assimilation because they separated Indigenous children from their families and Tribes and "Americanized" them while they were still malleable. However, not every boarding school was founded and operated for these purposes. In Alaska, for example, many Church-run boarding schools were created to shelter youth who were orphaned during epidemics or whose parents were experiencing illness or dire poverty and could not care for them.

---

* Dicasteries for Culture and Education and for Promoting Integral Human Development, *Joint Statement*, no. 6.

† The total number of Native boarding schools in the United States during the Boarding School Period (1819–1979) is estimated to be 408. During that period, there were a total of 84 boarding schools run by Catholic religious communities or Church entities, according to the website https://ctah.archivistsacwr.org/. Of those, the number of boarding schools that were entrusted by the federal government to Catholic church groups is estimated to be much lower, since a good number of them were created for assistance and educational purposes to poor and marginalized communities, outside of the government programs, and were funded by religious communities and their benefactors. Also, federal funding for Catholic boarding schools ended in the early 1900s.

Many Native alumni of those boarding schools who are still living today express gratitude for the care and educational opportunities they received from the men and women religious who administered mission schools. Many of these alumni used that formal education to launch successful careers and move into leadership positions across diverse fields. Regardless of the individual experiences at boarding schools, however, the system itself left a legacy of community and individual trauma that broke down family and support systems among Indigenous communities.

These multigenerational traumas continue to have an impact today, one that is perpetuated by racism and neglect of all kinds. Through our listening sessions, we heard that many Indigenous people feel unaccepted by and unwelcomed in society and even the Church. Further, Indigenous peoples still suffer disrespect and neglect within the larger U.S. society. It is no surprise, then, that historical trauma, systematic destruction of the Indigenous family, socioeconomic systems that perpetuate poverty in reservations, and a general lack of good educational opportunities all have led to extremely high rates of addiction and suicide among Native Americans even today. Of particular concern are Native youths and young adults, who register the highest rates of suicide among people of their age.[‡]

A LIVING TESTIMONY

The survival of Indigenous communities is a testament both to Indigenous Peoples' enduring strength and to the power of God's grace. Drawing upon their innately sacramental worldview and reverence for Creation, Indigenous Catholics in the United States have embraced the Gospel despite these tragic stories, which could easily have hardened their hearts against God and those in his Church. Healing and reconciliation can only take place when the Church acknowledges the wounds perpetrated on her Indigenous children and humbly listens as they voice their experiences.

The means by which our brothers and sisters heal from these trau-

---

[‡] Centers for Disease Control and Prevention, "Suicides Among American Indian/Alaska Natives — National Violent Death Reporting System, 18 States, 2003–2014," *Morbidity and Mortality Weekly Report* 67, no. 8 (March 2, 2018): 237–242, *dx.doi.org/10.15585/mmwr.mm6708a1.*

matic experiences, as well as how that healing takes place, should be led by Indigenous communities themselves. Finally, inculturation — the authentic, wholesome blending of faith and culture — should be a process of collaboration among Indigenous Catholics, Church leadership, and wider communities. This process must respect personal freedom and conscience while inviting Indigenous Catholics to discover the seeds of the Gospel already present in their cultures and to grow in their knowledge of God's love and his divinely revealed plan of salvation for all humankind. In the end, this process will convey a most important truth: that the Indigenous Peoples of the United States have a rightful place at the table of God.

PART TWO:

A Call to Mission

A RETURN TO AUTHENTIC EVANGELIZATION

In some parts of the world, the original process of evangelization accompanied colonization efforts. Honest missionary efforts to communicate the Gospel were often tarnished by the mistreatment of Indigenous people by settlers, colonizing powers, and even representatives of the Church. For some, this history has given rise to the idea that evangelization is just another form of oppressive colonialism.

However, the authentic Catholic approach to evangelization is predicated on the idea that all cultures are open to the truth of the Gospel. The Catholic Church teaches that within each culture is found goodness, planted there by God for the benefit of his children, a rich soil in which the Gospel can take root and bloom. As the Second Vatican Council's document on missionary activity, *Ad Gentes,** enunciated:

> Missionary activity makes Christ present, he who is the author of salvation. It purges of evil associations those elements of truth and grace which are found among peoples, and which are, as it were, a secret presence of God; and it restores them to Christ their source. … And so, whatever goodness is found in the minds and hearts of men, or in the particular customs and cultures of peoples, far from being lost, is purified, raised to a higher level and reaches its perfection, for the glory of God, the confusion of the demon, and the happiness of men. (9)
>
> The Church strictly forbids that anyone should be forced to accept the faith or be induced or enticed by unworthy devices; as it likewise strongly defends the right that no one should be frightened away from the faith by unjust persecutions. (13)
>
> [And also, the Church desires to] carefully consider how traditions of asceticism and contemplation, the seeds of which have been sown by God in certain ancient cultures before the preaching of the Gospel, might be incorporated into the Christian religious life. (18)

Centuries before the Second Vatican Council's constitution *Sacrosanctum*

---

* Decree on the Mission Activity of the Church, December 7, 1965.

Concilium and the Vatican instruction *Varietates Legitimae* addressed in-culturation,[†] Spanish Dominican Fr. Bartolomé de Las Casas (1488–1566) advocated to religious and secular authorities to promote the dignity and rights of Native Peoples. As a young man, Las Casas traveled to the West Indies, where he was revolted to witness the exploitation and physical abuse Indigenous Peoples suffered under Spanish conquerors. After undergoing a personal conversion, he gave up his own extensive land holdings and slaves and then returned to Spain repeatedly to petition the Spanish Crown to pass laws against the physical abuses of the Indigenous.[‡]

The concepts Las Casas developed were revolutionary for his time. He promoted and publicly defended the inherent dignity of Indigenous Peoples, spoke against the exploitive heart of colonialism, and called for enculturating the Gospel through a peaceful, Christlike invitation rather than through forced conversion. Drawing upon the works of St. Thomas Aquinas and Plato, Las Casas promoted a natural law basis for human rights that eventually found its way into the political systems of many nations.

Las Casas' ideas have taken centuries to influence nations. But God has always found ways, in the meantime, to affirm the dignity of Indigenous Peoples and their receptivity to the Gospel when it is presented as an invitation. In 1531, Our Lady of Guadalupe appeared as an Indigenous woman to an Indigenous man, St. Juan Diego Cuauhtlatoatzin, near present-day Mexico City, signaling that God embraces all his children, regardless of skin color, culture, or station in life. Through Our Lady of Guadalupe and through St. Juan Diego's testimony, millions of Indigenous Peoples of the Americas were led to embrace Catholicism. They were attracted to the faith because the Mother of God conveyed the message that God sees them, loves them, and wants them to thrive in this world and in the world to come.

Another saint whose life demonstrated the power of the Gospel to bloom in Native soil is St. Kateri Tekakwitha, the first Indigenous woman of the Americas to be recognized as a saint by the Catholic Church. St.

---

† See *Sacrosantum Concilium* (Constitution on the Sacred Liturgy), December 4, 1963, no. 123, *www.vatican.va /archive/hist_councils/ii_vatican_council/documents/vat-ii_const_19631204_sacrosanctum-concilium_en.html*; Congregation for Divine Worship and the Discipline of the Sacraments, *Varietates Legitimae* (Fourth Instruction for the Right Application of the Conciliar Constitution on the Liturgy, Nos. 37–40), March 29, 1994.

‡ See *The Pivotal Players Complete Special Edition*, episode 12, "Bartolomé de las Casas (2020)" (Washington, DC: Word on Fire Publishing, 2020), DVD.

Kateri was born in 1656 in what today is upstate New York, just nine years after the Jesuits St. Isaac Jogues, St. John de Brébeuf, and their companions were martyred by Iroquois warriors. Orphaned by smallpox, which also scarred her severely and left her partially blind, Kateri was baptized into the Catholic Church at age nineteen against the desires of her adoptive family.

The experience brought Saint Kateri closer to Christ but estranged her from her Indigenous family, many of whom associated Catholicism with oppressive French colonialism. Yet the young woman remained faithful to Christ, and to those who mistreated her she returned only love. Today, many Indigenous Catholics across the United States face similar crosses. Like Kateri, they strive to maintain their faith amid family members and a wider Tribal community who resent the Church due to past sins against their people. Kateri is a guide who can help Native Peoples meet profound suffering by seeking God's will through faith in Jesus Christ, connecting to his Church, and forgiving their persecutors.

We celebrate many other examples of Indigenous Peoples who willingly embraced the Gospel when missionaries offered it to them. Across these lands — from the Apalachee in Florida to the Yup'ik in Alaska, from the Mohawk in New York State to the Tohono O'odham in Arizona to the Osage in Oklahoma and the mission Indians of California — many Indigenous Peoples welcomed missionaries and received the Gospel with joy. In the 1800s, the Salish of Montana sent four delegations to St. Louis, asking for more "Black Robes." Many other Tribes requested Catholic missionaries. Since the beginning of the Church's missionary efforts here, Indigenous Peoples of these lands have recognized the truth of Jesus Christ and embraced his Church.

On the twenty-fifth anniversary of *Ad Gentes*, Pope St. John Paul II wrote his encyclical *Redemptoris Missio*,[*] in which he insisted that God fertilized every culture with sufficient beauty, goodness, and truth to receive the Gospel. Consequently, Indigenous Peoples have a right to be evangelized in and through their own cultures, in ways that respect their unique "nature and genius." This inculturation of faith will organically transform

---

[*] On the Permanent Validity of the Church's Missionary Mandate, December 7, 1990, *www.vatican.va/content /john-paul-ii/en/encyclicals/documents/hf_jp-ii_enc_07121990_redemptoris-missio.html.*

Indigenous communities over time.

Ad Gentes encouraged Indigenous Catholics to "give expression to this newness of life in the social and cultural framework of their own homeland, according to their own national traditions. They must be acquainted with this culture; they must heal it and preserve it; they must develop it in accordance with modern conditions, and finally perfect it in Christ, so that the Faith of Christ and the life of the Church are no longer foreign to the society in which they live, but begin to permeate and to transform it" (no. 21).

PART THREE:

A Call for Reconciliation

PASTORING NATIVE CATHOLICS

During his apostolic visit to the United States in 2015, Pope Francis canonized St. Junípero Serra in Washington, D.C. Following the Mass of the Canonization, the pope met with a group of California Native Americans descended from families who built each of the nine missions established by St. Junípero Serra. In a closed meeting, he listened to them, encouraged them, and assured them that he heard their concerns. In his homily that day, the Holy Father stated: "Junípero sought to defend the dignity of the native community, to protect it from those who had mistreated and abused it. Mistreatment and wrongs today still trouble us, especially because of the hurt which they cause in the lives of many people." The Church also desires to share this concern through a trauma-informed response to the wounds Indigenous members are currently suffering.[*]

In 2019, the Black and Indian Mission Office and the USCCB Subcommittee on Native American Affairs held a series of listening sessions in which Native Catholic leaders from throughout the country spoke to a group of nine bishops about issues their communities face.[†]

Additionally, in 2022 the Center for Applied Research in the Apostolate (CARA) and the USCCB's Subcommittee on Native American Affairs published a joint report titled *Catholic Native American Study*.[‡] The study describes the issues brought forward by Indigenous leaders, centered on the themes of healing and reconciliation, the family, the sacraments, social issues, and evangelization.

This Pastoral Framework discusses the first two themes in Part Three. Part Four covers the third theme, and Part Five discusses the last two.

HEALING AND RECONCILIATION

In 2021, Bishop James S. Wall, chairman of the USCCB Subcommittee on Native American Affairs, and Archbishop Paul S. Coakley, chairman of

---

[*] Pope Francis, Homily, Holy Mass and Canonization of St. Junípero Serra, Washington, DC, September 23, 2015, *www.vatican.va/content/francesco/en/homilies/2015/documents/papa-francesco_20150923_usa-omelia -washington-dc.html.*

[†] See, for example, Andy Orosco, "Listening Session 4: Importance of Acknowledging Past Wrongs Toward Indigenous People Associated with the California Mission System and a Better Explanation of the Canonization of St. Junípero Serra," 44–46, in Black and Indian Mission Office and the USCCB Subcommittee on Native American Affairs, *Listening Session,* March 2019, Phoenix.

[‡] CARA and USCCB Subcommittee on Native American Affairs, *Catholic Native American Study,* January 2022, Washington, DC.

the USCCB Committee on Domestic Peace, Justice, and Human Development, wrote to the bishops of the United States encouraging them to engage in dialogue with their local Native and Indigenous communities as a meaningful step toward the ongoing journey of healing and reconciliation. A sense of trust must first be cultivated before the Church's desire for reconciliation with the Native American community can be met. A similar desire for reconciliation on the part of the Native American community is also needed. The bishops recommended ways the U.S. bishops and local Catholic communities could rebuild trust with Indigenous Americans with respect to the history of Indigenous boarding schools operated by members of the Catholic Church. Their recommendations are applicable to Native American communities throughout the United States:

> Transparency — Where possible, locate historical information about the boarding schools, graves of Indigenous Americans, and other issues related to the treatment of Indigenous Americans by members of the Church, and make that information accessible to the public. Similarly, the Church should provide Native Peoples opportunities to examine their own sacramental records from reservations and missions. Moreover, diocesan bishops should consider enacting particular law governing older sacramental records.§ These historic records can provide important links to Native Peoples and their ancestors.

> Relationship building — Reach out to Indigenous Catholics and other Indigenous Americans to foster a trusting relationship and engage them in initiatives that address common concerns.

> Listening — Develop a process to conduct listening sessions with Indigenous communities at national and local levels. The process

---

§ Canonically, the general principle governing sacramental records is that they are to be carefully safeguarded (see c. 535 §4 CIC). Information contained in the records is provided to the individuals who have a right to the information — for example, to clarify their own canonical status or the status of persons under their legitimate care (see c. 487 §2, CIC). Regarding "older sacramental registers," canon law states that they are "also to be carefully protected," and they are to be governed by the "prescripts of particular law" (c. 535 §5, CIC), which each diocesan bishop has the authority to adopt. Therefore, a legitimate diversity in practice regarding access to older sacramental records can be found among different dioceses.

should include Elders, some of whom had experience with board-ing schools, reservations and missions, and also youths and other adult Indigenous Catholics who continue to experience racism, discrimination, and estrangement from our faith.

Accountability — All members of the Church should be open to cooperating with Tribal and other government investigations into any Catholic involvement in ethnic abuse. These investigations in-clude, but are not limited to, conduct at Native boarding schools.

Based upon these recommendations, we desire to accompany the Indige-nous Peoples in our dioceses by hearing from them directly. We commit to setting up listening sessions with Native Catholics and, if applicable and welcome, with Tribal leadership from Native lands that fall within our di-ocesan boundaries. Additionally, we commit to dedicating resources nec-essary to provide training for clergy, religious, and lay leaders to better minister to the pastoral needs of Indigenous Peoples. We want to facilitate increased understanding of one another by listening to Indigenous needs and concerns as a way to help all of us move toward greater reconciliation and healing.*

We also want to partner with ministries such as Catholic Charities and others that provide counseling and support groups for Indigenous Peoples who struggle with woundedness from trauma. At the national, diocesan, Tribal, and parish levels, we all must do our part to increase awareness and break the culture of silence that surrounds all types of afflictions and past mistreatment and neglect.

More than anything, the Church desires to demonstrate a commit-ment to encouraging Native Peoples to share their experiences to educate and enliven parishes. In recent years, a persistent theme has emerged in virtually all communications between church leadership and Native Cath-olics: when Indigenous Catholics speak, they need to be heard and under-stood by their shepherds and by the larger church family. Indigenous Cath-olics very much want to learn how to teach and defend the Catholic faith

---

* See Helen McClenahan, "Native Boarding Schools: Learn from History to Promote Healing, Speaker Says," *Northwest Catholic*, October 27, 2022, *nwcatholic.org/news/helen-mcclenahan/native-boarding-schools-learn-from-history-to-promote-healing-speaker-says*.

so they can evangelize their own peoples. Further, we see their desire to communicate their experiences and culture to the wider Church. They also want assurance that the Church will support them and will welcome their voices and contributions. Such support and welcome will help non-Indigenous Catholics better understand Native cultures and foster more inclusive faith communities.

THE FAMILY

For thousands of years, Indigenous communities have expressed how sacred it is when a man and a woman profess their love together. From this bonding of love and compassion, the Indigenous family has been a source of strength and resilience throughout history. The family is a traditional source grounding what is spiritual and good among all its members.

In Catholic teaching, the family is likewise the first place where God is worshiped and faith is practiced. In addition to serving as the foundation and school of faith, Indigenous families are the most important threads in the rich fabric that makes up Indigenous cultures. Indigenous families pass on their rich traditions and cultural aspects from one generation to the next.

A celebration of the Order of Celebrating Matrimony, for instance, might incorporate Indigenous cultural elements that emphasize the spiritual nature of both the wedding ceremony and the marriage. Including these cultural elements helps the spouses and their community connect faith and culture. The rich cultural symbols also strengthen the bonds within family, clan, and Tribe.

The Church desires to support Indigenous spouses and help couples marry in the Church. A new model for marriage preparation — one that features more direct mentorship and addresses specific issues that Indigenous couples face — should be developed to help them recognize the grace that flows from sacramental marriage in the Church and to prepare them to face together any marital issues that arise. Each Indigenous community has its own traditions with respect to marriage. Many have expressed a desire to incorporate those cultural traditions that are compatible with Catholic doctrine and the liturgical norms and practices into marriage preparation and into the wedding ceremony itself.

Native Catholic leaders should be employed to develop these programs and resources. Providing culturally appropriate counseling to individuals and couples, as well as other structures of support, will help spouses recognize when and where they need help.

Because the family is crucial to the health, happiness, and stability of every community, the Church — along with Tribal leaders and even government agencies — has a vested interest in supporting the long-term commitment of love, respect, and mutual support between husband and wife. This social dimension of marriage is an important focus of the Church's advocacy. The endurance of marriage and family is important not only for the spiritual life but also for the well-being of Indigenous communities. Such endurance is also an important way to combat poverty, racism, and many other social evils. We must also understand that, for Indigenous communities, the concept of family goes beyond the nuclear family to encompass the extended family, clan, and Tribe.

Native cultures esteem and value their Elders, especially the matriarchs of families. One example is Mary Kummagaq Kamkoff of the Yup'ik, as explained by Dr. Stephen "Walkie" Charles, professor and director of the Alaska Native Language Center:

Mary had the gift of knowing her "heart language," the Yup'ik language, as well as the English language, which was very rare to find in the region at the time. She had learned English while in the care of some missionaries who treated her for tuberculosis, which unfortunately had devastated the region in the early 1900s. Rev. Martin J. Lonneux, SJ, joined the Yup'ik people of northern Alaska in the early 1930s. Father Lonneux worked with Mary to create a writing system for the Yup'ik people of the region. It has been more than eighty years, and still today, the Catholic Yup'ik of northern Alaska pray and honor God and the Church "with prayers gifted to us by Mary Kummagaq Kamkoff and Father Martin Lonneux," say the people's Elders.*

---

* Cellam Yua, or the spirit of the universe, is recognized by the Yukon River delta Yup'ik people in Alaska. The Yup'ik/Cup'ik of Alaska know it by other names, such as Ellam Yua and Cillam Cua, and the Inupiaq people know this spirit as Silam Inua. Professor Stephen "Walkie" Charles, Ph.D., summary of written interview, January 19, 2023, University of Alaska, Fairbanks, Alaska.

Along with love and respect for Elders, attention to Native youths and young adults is an urgent matter. Repeatedly, Indigenous young people have spoken about a lack of hope. The high rate of suicide among younger generations of Indigenous People seems to corroborate that finding. Many feel disconnected from their culture and from the Church. They deal with issues at home that make them feel misunderstood and uncared for. They appreciate it when Elders take the time to teach them traditional Native values like prayer, respect for Elders and others, caring, honesty, generosity, humility, and wisdom. Experience shows how much identity formation hinges on passing on cultural values, traditions, and Native languages.

However, the breakdown of family and support systems often interferes with the passing down of traditional values. Some young people leave family and Tribal environments to seek educational or work opportunities elsewhere. This also contributes to cultural alienation.

Historical traumas are a significant contributor to the breakdown of family life among many Indigenous Peoples. In response, youth and young adults are disaffiliating from the institutional authorities such as the Church, community, and their Elders. Many have rejected Christianity and turned to pre-Christian Indigenous religious practices. Many long for belonging and acceptance and might find solace in social media and other outlets.

To fight this hopelessness, the Church recognizes a need for the revival of family life, meaningful community involvement, and investment in healing intergenerational trauma. When initiatives or programs require too many resources, materials, and personnel, it can be difficult to sustain these efforts at a mission church, a Native Catholic center in an urban setting, or a parish with limited finances. Dioceses/eparchies, parishes, and Catholic organizations dedicated to fostering ministries with youths and young adults should consider creative ways to engage Indigenous young people and train pastoral leaders with the tools they need to accompany these populations. Additionally, the Church should seek out pathways for Indigenous Catholic youth and young adults to become "protagonists of this transformation"[†] in developing such initiatives.

---

† Pope Francis, *Christus Vivit*, no. 174.

An example of good work being done with Native young people is the youth ministry at St. Francis Xavier Mission in South Dakota's Rosebud Reservation, home to Sicangu Sioux, a Tribe of Lakota:

> St. Francis Mission provides programs for basic re-evangeliza-
> tion of the Catholic population … religious education, recovery
> programs, programs that support Lakota language and culture.
> These are foundational requirements for leadership at Rosebud.
> To provide an educated and ethically responsible group of lead-
> ers, in the long term, St. Francis Mission must also provide a
> quality Catholic education.*

Sapa Un Catholic Academy is part of the evangelization work. Based on the "Nativity model" of schools, which has a proven track record among high-risk populations of producing students who are able to graduate from colleges and universities, Sapa Un is unique in that it requires students to learn Lakota language and culture in a Catholic context. St. Francis Mission also has a vibrant religious education program. It is unique in being able to hold release-time religion classes during the school day. Mission staff teach at three different schools, and St. Francis youth ministry participants are involved with community activities and collaborate with Tribal programs.

Another example of a best practice for engaging Catholic Native young adults is found in the USCCB *Journeying Together* process of intercultural dialogue from 2020 to 2023. By listening to and working with Catholic young adults from Indigenous communities (among other cultural communities), by working with those who minister among them, and by allowing them to lead intercultural dialogue sessions, we have learned about the needs and concerns of Catholic Native young adults — and about how better to respond to them. Through this process, the USCCB has been able to identify and encourage these young adults to carry out leadership roles as young prophetic voices within

---

* St. Francis Mission Among the Lakota, "Sapa Un Catholic Academy," accessed April 17, 2023, *sfmission.org/ sapa-un-catholic-academy.*

their communities and the larger Church.[†]

Like any other cultural family, Indigenous Peoples need support, fellowship, and community to persevere in their faith. However, some have expressed that the fellowship and community they seek are not currently found in the parish communities where they live or attend Mass. Church communities need to offer family support structures for Indigenous Peoples. We encourage priests, permanent deacons, men and women religious, others in consecrated life, as well as lay teachers, catechists, and adults to seek out and accompany Indigenous Peoples, particularly young people. By the ministry and guidance of these adults, we know that many Indigenous men and women may be open to hearing God's call to their vocation and mission in life through marriage, priesthood, diaconate, consecrated life, or lay ecclesial ministry.

Traditionally, many priests and consecrated sisters and brothers, working hand in hand with Native Elders, served as spiritual leaders. As bishops we have heard from some Native leaders that their communities feel a deep sense of loss in the current lack of priests and religious to live and work among them. We also encourage the promotion of Native catechists for these communities. Therefore, we encourage local church leaders to seek out lay men and women to step into ecclesial service and ministry alongside those who are ordained and consecrated, and that this investment be a pastoral priority for the evangelization and accompaniment of God's people.

---

† See USCCB Committee on Cultural Diversity in the Church, *Journeying Together: Intracultural and Intercultural Proceedings Report* (Washington, DC: USCCB, 2022), pp. 25–28, *www.usccb.org/resources /Journeying%20Together%20Proceedings%20Report%20May%209%202022_0.pdf.*

PART FOUR:

A Call to Holiness

SACRAMENTS AND WORSHIP

Sacraments, worship, and popular piety can play a central role in religious formation of Native Peoples when proper celebrations according to the Church are connected with Indigenous sensibilities and cultures.

It is important to remember Native American communities were the first to share in sacramental celebrations in the Americas and have helped to inform and shape many forms of popular worship today.

Sacramental preparation provides an excellent opportunity to deepen evangelization and catechesis among Indigenous Peoples. As Native families approach the Church to receive the sacraments, an extended conversation on matters of faith and life will help them better understand Church teachings and the implications of living life according to the Gospel, and will strengthen their relationships with Christ and one another.

For many Native communities, both healing rituals and those honoring the dead are meaningful. The Church can use these beliefs to deepen Indigenous understanding of how Christ is present and active in the sacraments. Through embracing the sacraments, many communities have experienced the profound hope of reconciliation, healing, and eternal life.

We all need authentic inculturation in the liturgy to deepen our relationship with Christ. The Church must emphasize the gift of all our senses — including sound, smell, taste, sight, and touch — so that celebrating the sacraments becomes a means to teach the tenets of the faith. In all cases, the inculturation of the liturgy must conform to the directives of the Holy See, the episcopal conference, and the diocesan bishop. At the same time, traditional rituals that complement and are compatible with Catholic doctrine and liturgical practices enhance the prayer life and religious experience of the people.

SACRED MUSIC

The liturgy should evoke both the loud voice and the whisper of God: "I heard a sound from heaven like the sound of rushing water or a loud peal of thunder. The sound I heard was like that of harpists playing their harps" (Rv 14:2).

Music and singing have always played a central role in worship for

Native Peoples and the Church alike. The Second Vatican Council recognized: "In certain parts of the world, especially mission lands, there are peoples who have their own musical traditions, and these play a great part in their religious and social life. For this reason, due importance is to be attached to their music, and a suitable place is to be given to it, not only in forming their attitude toward religion, but also in adapting worship to their native genius."* Singing is particularly appealing to Indigenous Americans, because singing recalls cultural ceremonies while moving people's hearts toward worshiping God. For example, bells or traditional instruments like gourds, drums, and clapping sticks can be used at the moment of consecration to draw the ear to the importance of the moment. Language is central to preserving cultural identities, so when approved by the Church, Native languages can also be incorporated judiciously at Mass, such as in the preaching and the prayers of the faithful, and in other celebrations of the Sacraments.

As the Congregation for Divine Worship and the Discipline of the Sacraments explained in *The Directory on Popular Piety and the Liturgy*:

> The adaptation or inculturation of a particular pious exercise should not present special difficulties at the level of language, musical and artistic forms, or even of adopting certain gestures. While at one level pious exercises do not concentrate on the essential elements of the sacramental life, at another, it has to be remembered, they are in many cases popular in origin and come directly from the people, and have been formulated in the language of the people, within the framework of the Catholic faith. ...
>
> It is especially necessary to ensure that those pious exercises undergoing adaptation or inculturation retain their identity and their essential characteristics. In this regard, particular attention must always be given to their historical origin and to the doctrinal and cultic elements by which they are constituted.†

---

* *Sacrosanctum Concilium*, no. 119.

† See Congregation for Divine Worship and the Discipline of the Sacraments, *The Directory on Popular Piety and the Liturgy*, no. 92, https://www.vatican.va/roman_curia/congregations/ccdds/documents/rc_con_ccdds_doc_20020513_vers-direttorio_en.html.

SACRAMENTALS

Sacramentals are another important way to connect with cultural elements that evoke the Divine. Some Tribal communities have traditionally used sacred smoke as a purifying element to offer prayers, and as a way to recognize the presence of the Divine. As the psalmist writes, "Let my prayer be incense before you; / my uplifted hands an evening offering" (Ps 141:2). Therefore, the regular use of incense is encouraged in the Mass and other sacred rituals celebrated among Native faith communities. Likewise, because of its aroma, we encourage generous use of sacred chrism when the Sacred Liturgy calls for it, especially in baptism and ordinations, and in the dedication of churches and altars. Holy water provides a powerful connection with the elements of nature. Also, blessed salt could be used in blessings and other rituals.

All sacramentals and elements used in the sacramental rites should be fully explained, to draw the minds and bodies of Indigenous worshipers into deeper understanding of the Catholic faith. These explanations should take place in solid catechetical instruction. In this way, true inculturation and authentic evangelization are achieved. The Catholic faith has been readily accepted by many Indigenous Peoples because of the rich symbolism of our faith connected with their own cultures. Indigenous Peoples have an innately sacramental worldview, as noted earlier, which acknowledges material creation as a pathway for recognizing the divine Creator and corresponds to the Catholic sacramental principle.

SACRED SPACES AND IMAGES

In many areas, Native Peoples, with Catholic missionaries, are responsible for the most significant sustained construction of Catholic sacred sites throughout the Americas. In many cases, our historic churches are the only visible landmarks associated with Native Peoples. Because of this, these spaces are sacred for many reasons. Cultivating a pastoral sensitivity and awareness of the contribution of Native Peoples to the founding of many Catholic communities across the United States is essential when seeking a pastoral relationship with regional Natives. These holy places, built by the hands of Native Peoples, remain, in many examples, the spiritual and economic heart of the community. Indigenous People's remarkable contribution to our faith has served generations of Catholics from all over the world.

The orientation of Catholic church buildings offers an opportunity to connect to the importance that some Native communities assign to the four directions: east, south, west, and north.[*] For example, many Catholic churches are oriented so that the altar is to the east, since we traditionally look to the Risen Christ in the East.[†] This Catholic practice finds an echo in the Navajo belief that houses should be built with the front door facing the East, toward the rising sun of the new day.

Ideally, the construction of churches and chapels will reflect connections between Church requirements and cultural practices. Psalm 123 declares, "To you I raise my eyes, / to you enthroned in heaven" (v. 1). The church building should be a space set apart from the mundane and designed to draw people's eyes to heaven. It should be beautifully adorned with images relevant to the people it serves. Such adornment could include images of saints of great importance to the congregation.[‡] As the Second Vatican Council tells us:

> The Church has not adopted any particular style of art as her very own; she has admitted styles from every period according to the natural talents and circumstances of peoples, and the needs of the various rites. Thus, in the course of the centuries, she has brought into being a treasury of art which must be very carefully preserved. The art of our own days, coming from every race and region, shall also be given free scope in the Church, provided that it adorns the sacred buildings and holy rites with due reverence and honor; thereby it is enabled to contribute its own voice to that wonderful chorus of praise in honor of the Catholic faith sung by great men in times gone by.[§]

---

[*] Many Indigenous communities use the Four Directions to orient themselves to the Divine. See Tekakwitha Conference, "Prayer in Four Directions," accessed April 17, 2023, *tekconf.org/prayer-in-four-directions*.

[†] See Pope St. John Paul II, *Orientale Lumen* (*Apostolic Letter to Mark the Centenary of Orientalium Dignitas* of Pope Leo XIII), May 2, 1995, no. 28, *www.vatican.va/content/john-paul-ii/en/apost_letters/1995/documents/hf_jp -ii_apl_19950502_orientale-lumen.html*.

[‡] The Cathedral of the Madeline in the Diocese of Salt Lake City houses a remarkable set of Native American style Stations of the Cross.

[§] *Sacrosantum Concilium*, no. 123.

As bishops, we encourage local churches to engage Indigenous artists when commissioning sacred art and iconography for churches and chapels, especially in communities where Indigenous groups have a significant presence.

THE EUCHARIST

The liturgy is "the summit toward which the activity of the Church is directed, and at the same time the font from which all her power flows" (*Sacrosanctum Concilium*, 10). Above all, the liturgy of the Eucharist provides the primary source for healing, evangelization, reconciliation, holiness, and transformation as proposed in this document. The goal to 'keep Christ's sacred promise will come to fruition through our participation in the Eucharist.

Strong emphasis should be placed on the Real Presence of Christ in the celebration of the Eucharist, in which we receive the body and blood of Jesus Christ. No truth is more powerful or beautiful than the fact that the Eucharist unites us to the body, blood, soul, and divinity of Christ in a real and tangible way. Jesus tells us: "Amen, amen, I say to you, unless you eat the flesh of the Son of Man and drink his blood, you do not have life within you. Whoever eats my flesh and drinks my blood has eternal life, and I will raise him on the last day. For my flesh is true food, and my blood is true drink" (John 6:53–55).

Catholic Native Peoples have a deep reverence for and devotion to the mystery of Christ's Real Presence in the Eucharist. In general, Indigenous communities demonstrate an innate capacity to accept and integrate into their cultural beliefs this mystical union of the human and the divine, of matter and spirit.

Let us not forget that the sacraments, especially the Eucharist, also serve as a prime opportunity for the Church to help heal past wounds. Through the grace of the sacraments, the Holy Spirit provides ways to open the heart as a necessary part of the healing process. We urge a renewed focus on catechesis and faith formation to help all generations of Indigenous Catholics know and love their faith.

RELIGIOUS EDUCATION

Indigenous Peoples have shown a great desire for more catechetical instruction. Church leaders have various means to satisfy the right and obligation of Indigenous Peoples to a Christian education. Catholic schools continue to be an effective way to provide religious education, despite low budgets and minimal staff. A Catholic school or even just an after-school program can be successful, no matter how big or small, so long as it forms missionary disciples. This formation can be accomplished by focusing primarily on deep prayer life and on the richness of the sacraments. The Church should also reassess how we teach youths, realizing that the Western style of classroom education does not always work best for Native learning.

Indigenous Peoples have strong oral traditions, and storytelling is a traditional way for Elders to anchor the younger generation to the past as a solid foundation for the future. This highly effective, traditional method of transmitting faith and culture has been lost in many Indigenous communities. Catholic schools and religious education programs, especially among the young, should encourage and support developing and reviving oral means of transmitting the faith.

There are many Native American traditions, practices, and beliefs that complement and are parallel to Catholic doctrine and that facilitate instruction in the faith. Among these are the recognition of a single God, the Creator, the inspiration of the Spirit, water as a source of cleansing and rebirth, the sacramental nature of creation, and the continuation of life after death.

Finally, local churches in collaboration with Native leaders should offer training in cultural sensitivity toward Native Peoples for clergy, consecrated religious and those in formation, seminarians, and lay ecclesial ministers, with special emphasis on and attention to the Indigenous communities being served by the diocese/eparchy or other local Catholic communities.

PART FIVE:

A Call of Transformation

SOCIAL ISSUES

During one of the bishops' listening sessions with Catholic Native leaders, Ben Black Bear III, of the Sicangu Lakota, talked about his experience working for the Rosebud Reservation in South Dakota: "There are many families who do not have a steady income to provide their basic needs such as food, clothing, and a safe and comfortable home. The poverty on the reservation is devastating and there is a true need for various types of help and support."[*]

Social issues perpetuate the cycle of generational trauma that many Indigenous Peoples experience. The Church in the United States must discern how best to allocate resources to support Indigenous communities in need.

While some Native communities are economically self-sufficient, many others experience economic deprivation. Recently, the Church has renewed efforts to study the causes of poverty, create strategies to combat social and economic injustice, and provide resources to ensure that Native communities can provide for those in need.

One example of how the Church can address social issues and injustices facing Native American communities centers on recommendations from the 2019 Reservation Anti-Poverty Summit.[†] At the University of Notre Dame, the USCCB Subcommittee on Native American Affairs hosted a gathering of experts on poverty, education, and community development in Native reservations. At the end of the meeting, participants made recommendations in several areas.

1. NATURAL RESOURCES

In many cases natural resources are misused and do not benefit the Native Peoples who live on the land. "This is especially clear when planning economic activities which may interfere with Indigenous cultures and their ancestral relationship to the earth. In this regard, the right to prior and informed consent should always prevail, as foreseen in Article 32 of the Declaration on the Rights of Indigenous Peoples. Only then is it pos-

---

[*] "Listening Session 1: Poverty and Social Issues," 4, Black and Indian Mission Office and the USCCB Subcommittee on Native American Affairs, *Listening Session,* Phoenix, 2019.

[†] USCCB Subcommittee on Native American Affairs, "Reservation Anti-Poverty Summit", October 2019, Notre Dame, IN. (Unpublished draft of recommendations, February 11, 2020)

sible to guarantee peaceful cooperation between governing authorities and indigenous peoples, overcoming confrontation and conflict," Pope Francis said in his greeting to Indigenous participants in the 2017 International Agricultural Development Forum.[‡]

Concerns About the Changing Environment

Native communities who are dependent upon the land, the seas, and the rivers are especially vulnerable to environmental changes. Every year, drought, wildfires, flooding, and blizzards add to the financial and personal toll paid by many Indigenous Peoples whose livelihoods depend on reservation land.[§]

Further, many Native communities are dependent on the natural resources within reservations, including water and mineral wealth. Leaders identified a continuing need for wise stewardship and partnership with Native authorities and leadership, so that continuing exploration and use of these resources avoid a high environmental cost.

As Pope Francis wrote in his encyclical *Laudato Si'* about the environment:

> It is essential to show special care for Indigenous communities and their cultural traditions. They are not merely one minority among others, but should be the principal dialogue partners, especially when large projects affecting their land are proposed. For them, land is not a commodity but rather a gift from God and from their ancestors who rest there, a sacred space with which they need to interact if they are to maintain their identity and values. When they remain on their land, they themselves care for it best. Nevertheless, in various parts of the world, pressure is being put on them to abandon their homelands to make room for agricultural or mining projects which

---

[‡] "The Pope Greets Representatives of Indigenous Peoples Participating in the Third Forum Held by the International Fund for Agricultural Development," Holy See Press Office, February 15, 2017, quoting from the U.N. Declaration on Rights of Indigenous Peoples, 2007, *www.press.vatican.va/content/salastampa/en/bollettino /pubblico/2017/02/15/170215a.html.*

[§] See National Wildlife Federation, *Facing the Storm: Indian Tribes, Climate-Induced Weather Extremes, and the Future for Indian Country* (Boulder, CO: National Wildlife Federation, 2011), 4–11, *www.nwf.org/~/media/PDFs /Global-Warming/Reports/TribalLands_ExtremeWeather_Report.ashx.*

are undertaken without regard for the degradation of nature and culture.*

2. HOUSING AND ACCESS TO FINANCING

The lack of adequate housing on many Native reservations is a big concern. This lack arises, in part, because many Native Americans do not meet the requirements to obtain home loans from traditional lending institutions. To develop and maintain housing loan programs, funding for Native Community Development Financial Institutions (CDFIs) must increase. Faith communities also need to develop an awareness of Native CDFIs.

The Catholic Campaign for Human Development (CCHD) has been at the forefront of developing and implementing CDFIs for the benefit of many Native communities. CCHD operates two grant programs for community development and economic development.† Since 1994, CCHD has provided more than $11 million in funding to dozens of Native-led organizations. Three such examples are as follows:

- **Citizen Potawatomi Nation Community Development Corporation — Shawnee, Oklahoma**

  Jason Glasgow's construction firm (Glasgow Paving) received much-needed new equipment when it joined a growing number of Native American-owned businesses securing loans from the CCHD-funded Citizen Potawatomi Nation Community Development Corporation (CDC). The Potawatomi Nation set up this CDC in 2003 to provide business development services and make commercial and consumer loans to Tribal members and other Native Americans across the United States. The Citizen Potawatomi Nation CDC also provides financial education to Tribal members.

---

* *Laudato Si'* (On Care for Our Common Home), May 24, 2015, no. 146, *www.vatican.va/content/francesco/en /encyclicals/documents/papa-francesco_20150524_enciclica-laudato-si.html*.

† USCCB Catholic Campaign for Human Development, "Economic Development Grants: Community-Development Financial Institutions," accessed April 17, 2023, *www.usccb.org/about/catholic-campaign-for-human -development/grants/economic-development-grants-program/upload/community-development-financial -institutions.pdf*.

- **Four Bands Community Fund — Eagle Butte, South Dakota**

In the area served by the Four Bands Community Fund, only 1 percent of businesses are owned by Native Americans, but Native Americans make up nearly 80 percent of the population. Four Bands incorporated in April 2000 to lend money to businesses and entrepreneurs who are Tribal members. The organization takes its name from the Four Bands of Native Peoples living in their reservation. The Four Bands Community Fund provides training, technical assistance, marketing support, and access to Made on the Rez, a retail and e-commerce business that sells Native-made products. Participants can receive microloans of up to $5,000 or can qualify for larger, revolving small business loans of up to $50,000. As part of the larger loans, Cheyenne River Entrepreneurial Assistance Training and Education courses guide members by teaching personal finance, business planning, and the basics of writing a business plan. In an area with some of the highest poverty rates in the country, Four Bands Community Fund is helping residents to feel pride in their accomplishments and to hope for self-sufficiency.

- **Thunder Valley Community Development Corporation — South Dakota**

Oglala Lakota established Thunder Valley Community Development Corporation to build sustainable communities. Thunder Valley CDC, which has received grant funding from CCHD, has the overall mission to "empower low-income Lakota youth and families to improve the health, culture, and environment of their communities through affordable housing, youth leadership, social enterprise, Lakota language [classes], food sovereignty, [and] workforce development, and to create systemic change through partnerships with a variety of organizations and stakeholders in the region."*

These examples should encourage Catholics and others to support microlending opportunities and programs that reinforce Native agency in developing and improving their local communities.

3. EDUCATION

The lack of access to a quality education for some Natives perpetuates a cycle of unemployment and underemployment. Catholic schools are a beacon of hope, but they only serve a small portion of Native American youth.

Resources need to be developed to address the scarcity of Indigenous teachers; these initiatives should include training, incentives to work with Native youth, and other ways to help educators. We encourage Catholic universities to respond to the needs of Indigenous teachers. An important recommendation from the 2019 anti-poverty summit was to develop a teacher recruitment program focusing on Native Americans by using stories and inspiration from Native teachers. Further, summit participants identified a need for a rigorous academic curriculum that is still culturally responsive and for a rigorous national standard curriculum that includes language and cultural elements, such as those currently being implemented by the American Indian Catholic Schools Network (AICSN).†

In California, for instance, the state-mandated curriculum for third and fourth grades requires instruction about Native People and the missions. In the wake of the canonization of St. Junípero Serra, the bishops of California made a commitment to Native California Indians to ensure that the history taught in Catholic schools and parishes and at the missions is factual, accurate, and complete. The bishops facilitated, together with historical experts, educators, and Native representatives, a revised curriculum for use by Catholic schools and institutions. These efforts

---

* Beth Griffin, "Thunder Valley Community Development Corporation," *Helping People Help Themselves*, no. 1 (2017), 1, *www.usccb.org/about/catholic-campaign-for-human-development/upload/cchd-nl-17-1-thundervalley. pdf.*

† See AICSN website at *ace.nd.edu/programs/aicsn.*

will continue to be assessed in cooperation with Native communities.

Finally, local parishes may consider access to educational opportunities for local Native children.

4. HEALTH CARE

Indigenous communities face several health disparities, including increased risks of chronic liver disease, diabetes mellitus, accidental injuries, assault and homicide, suicide, and chronic lower respiratory diseases.[‡] As a result, the life expectancy for Native Americans is five years shorter than that of non-Indigenous. To address these disparities, Catholic health providers across the country continue to partner with and support Native communities and develop programs to assist them. This work includes programs to improve cancer prevention, treatments, and cure rates for Indigenous Peoples in the Northern Plains; partnerships with the Great Plains Tribal Chairmen's Health Board to provide health education; COVID-19 vaccination and treatment outreach programs; partnerships with the federal government's Indian Health Service to provide telehealth services on reservations; and the creation of the American Indian Health Initiative in South Dakota as a venue for listening and partnering with Tribal leaders.[§] In addition, Catholic hospitals are working to improve maternal, infant, and pediatric care for Native Americans.

Local Catholic communities can partner with the Catholic Health Association system and other entities to improve the health of Native Americans in their midst.

5. RACISM

Racism is an intergenerational scourge that continues to affect Native Peoples — a scourge that compounds so many other social ailments affecting them. As we wrote in our 2018 pastoral letter *Open Wide Our Hearts,* "the effects of this evil remain visible in the great difficulties experienced by Native American communities today. Poverty, unemploy-

---

‡ See Indian Health Service, "Indian Health Disparities," October 2019, accessed February 28, 2023, *www.ihs.gov/ sites/newsroom/themes/responsive2017/display_objects/documents/factsheets/Disparities.pdf.*

§ See Avera Health, "Avera American Indian Health Initiative," accessed February 29, 2023, *www.avera.org/rural-health-initiative/american-indian-health-initiative;* Julie Minda, "Indigenous People Have Fared Far Worse in Pandemic than White People," *Catholic Health World,* May 1, 2021, *www.chausa.org/publications/catholic-health-world/article/may-1-2021/indigenous-people-have-fared-far-worse-in-pandemic-than-caucasians.*

ment, inadequate health care, poor schools, the exploitation of natural resources, and disputes over land ownership are all factors that cannot, and should not, be ignored."*

By promoting and developing intercultural competence, the Church can challenge negative stereotypes and emphasize the positive contributions of Indigenous Peoples in the Church and society.

6. CONCERNS OF URBAN NATIVES

As bishops of the United States, we recognize that the majority of Indigenous Peoples in the country reside outside reservations. We want to develop ministries that reach Native communities and individuals wherever they reside.

The needs of the Native American population on reservations and our ministry to them is a pressing concern. They are often the most neglected and overlooked citizens of our nation and our Church. But we must also care for the large urban Native population. Seven of ten Native American are urban Indians, many of whom have lost all ties to the reservations but still experience the traumas of their history.

Pastorally, it is also essential to understand regional dynamics. The displacement and migration of Native Peoples due to reservations, boarding schools, and other circumstances have led to many Native People residing outside of their traditional lands. Awareness of Native Peoples' history in a given region is important to understand and is sometimes neglected in discussions.

Additionally, pastoral awareness and sensitivity are needed in understanding regional dynamics as not all Native Peoples belong to a state or federally recognized Tribe or Band. In this way, the Church offers a unique place of acknowledgment to all Indigenous People.

Many Indigenous Peoples have found economic and educational opportunities in urban centers and have contributed positively to regional government and are thriving. Yet many others, facing impoverished conditions in rural areas, have left for urban areas only to find deprivation there, too. In cities around the United States, church and community organizations are working for the physical and spiritual support of Na-

---

* USCCB, *Open Wide Our Hearts*, p.12.

tive communities residing there. These programs provide food, primary health care, housing assistance, legal services, job-seeking and Native art training programs, and opportunities for members to engage in culturally meaningful community-building activities. Some also work to prevent or alleviate Native American homelessness. We advocate for programs that integrate Native languages, cultural elements, and traditions as ways to improve self-awareness, strengthen Indigenous identity, and contribute positively to healing and social transformation.

EVANGELIZATION
The Catholic Church in the United States has a rich history of Indigenous Catholics with enduring faith who have set examples of holiness for the entire community of believers. Many early Indigenous converts to Catholicism faced persecution and even martyrdom for their beliefs, either within their own communities or from others outside their communities. The Martyrs of La Florida stand as shining examples of Native Americans who willingly died before they would renounce their faith in Christ. St. Kateri Tekakwitha was ostracized from her family for her Catholicism, yet she did not let go of the hope she found in her faith. What led these men and women to hold onto their faith despite persecution?

These Indigenous Catholics' natural attunement to the divine and their sense of the common good led them not just to communicate the Good News of salvation to their villages and Tribal communities, but also to defend their newfound dignity as children of God, even to the point of giving up their lives. Once an individual has had a true encounter with the person of Jesus Christ through the sacraments of the Church and the proclamation of the kerygma and has received proper instruction about the mysteries of the faith (catechesis), he or she finds it very difficult to renounce the truth of God's love for all humankind. This knowledge becomes a source of true joy and life — not just for these individuals but for their entire community.

The Church must empower Indigenous members by providing the necessary formation and resources to carry on their mission of evangelization. The Church today can learn from the strength, love, and zeal of the great missionaries to the Indigenous populations of this continent.

This learning connects the Church of today with the important mission work of the past. The truth about these great figures must be shared, especially amid a culture that seeks to discredit them. The inclusion of accurate histories of missionaries and their efforts with Native American communities as a part of our religious instruction today can also help to bring attention, open discussion, and provide opportunities to strengthen relationships with Native Peoples.

Programs should be established to form and allow ordained and lay missionaries once again to support the mission churches that minister among Indigenous communities. This call to mission needs to be accompanied by the development of opportunities for local Native leaders to share the faith within their communities.

With these programs, we must take special care to ensure that Native families are fully vested in being the domestic church. In its exercise of faith development, the family, especially the community Elders, has a special place in transmitting the knowledge of Christ as a precious gift to the next generation.

The Church must convey the truth that its doors are wide open to Native Peoples and their families. Like a loving mother, the Church must reach out constantly and creatively to her children, especially those most in need, and remind them that no one is hidden from the Father's loving and merciful gaze. Those lacking evangelization and instruction in their Catholic faith are often challenged when they encounter non-Catholic spiritualities that seek their attention.

Also, among Native communities can be found a significant movement to abandon Christianity and turn to traditional Indigenous religions. Many Native Catholics have shared with us that they are feeling this tension. Finding no adequate response to the diverse threats that challenge their beliefs, they seek a beacon to guide them to calmer seas. Only the Church can provide this light, who is Jesus himself. The Church must therefore increase efforts to evangelize and instruct Native Catholics, particularly by empowering Indigenous catechists, and must use as a lamp the bright example of holy Native men and women who have preceded us in the faith. Indigenous Peoples desire to have members of their community actively involved in Catholic ministry in their dioceses.

The most effective means of evangelization remains personal invitation. Outreach to inactive Catholics, those who are homebound or hospitalized, those who are imprisoned, and any Native Catholic who feels forgotten or abandoned is best accomplished when the Church trains Native Catholics and raises them into leadership positions in their parish community, as well as to the diaconate and the priesthood.

The Church realizes that helping Native Peoples heal from the intergenerational wounds that still affect them is an important part of its ministry and a means of evangelization. Through the Word of God and the sacramental life, a welcoming and supportive Christian community can facilitate a personal encounter with Christ for those who most need the Divine Physician's healing.

Conclusion

We conclude by repeating the words that St. John Paul II addressed to the Native Peoples of the Americas in 1987:

> I encourage you, as Native People belonging to the different tribes and nations in the East, South, West and North, to preserve and keep alive your cultures, your languages, the values and customs which have served you well in the past and which provide a solid foundation for the future. Your customs that mark the various stages of life, your love for the extended family, your respect for the dignity and worth of every human being, from the unborn to the aged, and your stewardship and care of the earth: these things benefit not only yourselves but the entire human family.
>
> Your gifts can also be expressed even more fully in the Christian way of life. The Gospel of Jesus Christ is at home in every people. It enriches, uplifts, and purifies every culture. All of us together make up the People of God, the Body of Christ, the Church. We should all be grateful for the growing unity, presence, voice, and leadership of Catholic Native Americans in the Church today.*

An unfortunate tension exists today for many Indigenous Catholics, who feel they are presented with a false choice: be Native or be Catholic. Some

---

* Pope John Paul II, *Address to the Native Peoples of the Americas*, no. 4; Phoenix, 1987, https://www.vatican.va/content/john-paul-ii/en/speeches/1987/september/documents/hf_jp-ii_spe_19870914_amerindi-phoenix.html, no. 4

believe an irreconcilable chasm exists between traditional Indigenous culture and Catholicism. For Native Catholics who feel this tension, we assure you, as the Catholic bishops of the United States, that you do not have to be one or the other. You *are* both. Your cultural embodiment of the faith is a gift to the Church.

This Pastoral Framework is one of several steps toward the revitalizing of Native Catholic ministry. This framework reflects ideas, values, and areas of importance that the bishops have noted in dialogue with Catholic Native leaders. This text is intended to be used by dioceses, parishes, regions, Native Catholic leaders, Catholic schools, and other Catholic institutions serving Indigenous populations to develop specific priorities, initiatives, and programs tailored to the needs, concerns, and aspirations of the local Native populations. We acknowledge the great diversity of Tribes, languages, and cultural traditions that exist among the Indigenous populations in the United States of America and its territories. We know that one size does not fit all and affirm that any pastoral plans of action need to start with Catholic Natives themselves and be developed at the local level.†

For our part at the U.S. Conference of Catholic Bishops, we will continue to meet with Native leadership to develop practical actions and suggestions to implement this Pastoral Framework. For this purpose, and in conjunction with the Black and Indian Mission Office, we commit to conduct a follow-up listening session with Catholic Native leaders within a year or so after the approval of this framework. Further, because their experiences differ from those of the other states, separate attention needs to be given to Alaskan Natives, Hawaiian Natives, and the California Mission Indians (given their unique historical experience) to formulate specific action plans that can be accomplished in the next few years to enhance and support their ministries, as well as to the Mayan communities (mostly from Guatemala) and other Indigenous Peoples of the Americas (such as the Purepechas from Mexico) who reside in the United States.

Also, there needs to be continued dialogue with experts and organi-

---

† See "Summary of Key Areas and Suggested Action Steps to Further Develop Native/Indigenous Ministry" at the end of this section.

zations to combat Native poverty, lack of access to health care and educational opportunities, and other factors that hinder Native Peoples' social progress and development.

Because the issue of the "doctrine of discovery" has had such a profound impact on the lives of Indigenous populations in many different countries, we suggest that there should be an international conference to study its history and consequences, so that the effects felt even today by many Indigenous communities can be understood.

Finally, the Catholic bishops must continue to work to promote healing and reconciliation with any Native communities that may have experienced mistreatment and trauma at institutions run by Catholic religious communities or organizations and expand this important healing work and ministry.

In the introduction to this Pastoral Framework, we expressed our sincere apology for the Church's failure to respond adequately to those entrusted to our pastoral care. But we must go beyond an apology to take concrete actions, if we are to restore trust within these communities and demonstrate our true willingness to be transparent, present, and accountable to them. As we listen to the voice of Indigenous Catholics and provide opportunities for them to share their experiences, we as a trauma-informed community must be careful not to dictate the process.

The Church in the United States needs its Native members to offer their gifts to the rest of the Church so that all may be mutually edified. Indigenous Peoples' courage, humility, and respect inspire the Church to hold firm in faith, hope, and charity through difficulties. The vast majority of Indigenous Peoples believe in the Spirit of the Creator. In a world that is increasingly secular, the Indigenous worldview — which recognizes that we are all created and loved by God — stands as a beacon of hope and truth. Indigenous Catholics witness to the rest of the Church about the need to see God in day-to-day life. In a culture consumed by materialism, Indigenous Peoples' focus on the supernatural is inspirational. The Church must use all available resources to evangelize and form this part of the Body of Christ. Native People themselves are best positioned to pass on the faith to their families, in imitation of the Indigenous holy men and women who have come before us.

We turn our prayers to Our Lady of Guadalupe, Star of the New Evangelization in the Americas, for her assistance as we journey together toward heaven. May she guide our hearts ever closer to her son, Jesus. May we be inspired by her words to St. Juan Diego: "Hear me and understand well, my little son, that nothing should frighten or grieve you. Let not your heart be disturbed. Do not fear that sickness, nor any other sickness or anguish. Am I not here, who am your mother? Are you not under my protection? Am I not your health? Are you not happily within my fold? What else do you wish? Do not grieve nor be disturbed by anything."*

May we never lose hope, assured of her love and care for us and especially for Indigenous Catholics, who are always in our hearts. May Jesus, who is the Way, the Truth, and the Life, guide our encounter with one another on our certain path to the heavenly homeland.

---

* See *Nican Mopohua,* the story of the apparitions of Our Lady of Guadalupe to the Indigenous man St. Juan Diego. Modified version from various translations.

SUMMARY OF KEY AREAS AND SUGGESTED AC-TION STEPS TO FURTHER DEVELOP NATIVE/IN-DIGENOUS MINISTRY

1. Develop a process for listening sessions with local Native communities.
2. Build relationships between dioceses, parishes, and Tribal leadership.
3. Where applicable, develop resources to help alleviate trauma associated with the boarding-school period.
4. Raise awareness of social justice issues and concerns affecting Native communities.
5. Develop ways to support and strengthen Native marriages and family life.
6. Work with healthcare professionals to develop programs that foster prevention of suicide and recovery from alcoholism and substance abuse, especially among the young.
7. Support initiatives that promote Native language and culture.
8. Focus on cultivating Native vocations.
9. Establish programs to educate priests, seminarians, religious men and women, and lay missionaries about Catholic Native cultures.
10. Educate seminarians for "intentional discipleship" by highlighting the relationship between evangelization and inculturation of the Gospel in the programs of formation in seminaries and religious houses of formation. In particular, create opportunities for seminarians to learn about and experience local Catholic Native cultures and traditions.
11. Develop catechetical and evangelization resources that are culturally appropriate.
12. Develop guidelines for authentic inculturation of the liturgy that incorporate Indigenous cultural elements in conformity with the directives of the Holy See, the episcopal conference, and the diocesan bishop.

13. Educate the wider Catholic community about Catholic Native ministry.
14. Develop ways to increase Native access to financing and microlending opportunities.
15. Help Catholic universities respond to the needs of Native teachers, including educational development opportunities.
16. Help local Native communities to partner with the Catholic Health Services and other local or regional community healthcare providers.
17. Call for or participate in an international forum where the history and consequences of what is known collectively as the "doctrine of discovery" can be studied and looked at in depth to understand its effects even today.

Appendix

Vatican Dicasteries for Culture and Education and for Promoting Integral Human Development Joint Statement on the "Doctrine of Discovery" (March 30, 2023)

1. In fidelity to the mandate received from Christ, the Catholic Church strives to promote universal fraternity and respect for the dignity of every human being.

2. For this reason, in the course of history the popes have condemned acts of violence, oppression, social injustice, and slavery, including those committed against Indigenous Peoples. There have also been numerous examples of bishops, priests, women and men religious, and lay faithful who gave their lives in defense of the dignity of those peoples.

3. At the same time, respect for the facts of history demands an acknowledgment of the human weakness and failings of Christ's disciples in every generation. Many Christians have committed evil acts against Indigenous Peoples for which recent Popes have asked forgiveness on numerous occasions.

4. In our own day, a renewed dialogue with Indigenous Peoples, especially with those who profess the Catholic Faith, has helped the Church to understand better their values and cultures. With their help, the Church has acquired a greater awareness of their sufferings, past and present, due to the expropriation of their lands, which they consider a sacred gift from God and their ancestors, as well as the policies of forced assimilation, promoted by the governmental authorities of the time, intended to eliminate their Indigenous cultures. As Pope Francis has emphasized, their sufferings constitute a powerful summons to abandon the colonizing mentality and to walk with them side by side, in mutual respect and dialogue, recognizing the rights and cultural values of all individuals and

peoples. In this regard, the Church is committed to accompany Indigenous Peoples and to foster efforts aimed at promoting reconciliation and healing.

5. It is in this context of listening to Indigenous Peoples that the Church has heard the importance of addressing the concept referred to as the "doctrine of discovery." The legal concept of "discovery" was debated by colonial powers from the sixteenth century onward and found particular expression in the nineteenth-century jurisprudence of courts in several countries, according to which the discovery of lands by settlers granted an exclusive right to extinguish, either by purchase or conquest, the title to or possession of those lands by Indigenous Peoples. Certain scholars have argued that the basis of the aforementioned "doctrine" is to be found in several papal documents, such as the bulls *Dum Diversas* (1452), *Romanus Pontifex* (1455), and *Inter Caetera* (1493).

6. The "doctrine of discovery" is not part of the teaching of the Catholic Church. Historical research clearly demonstrates that the papal documents in question, written in a specific historical period and linked to political questions, have never been considered expressions of the Catholic faith. At the same time, the Church acknowledges that these papal bulls did not adequately reflect the equal dignity and rights of Indigenous Peoples. The Church is also aware that the contents of these documents were manipulated for political purposes by competing colonial powers in order to justify immoral acts against Indigenous Peoples that were carried out, at times, without opposition from ecclesiastical authorities. It is only just to recognize these errors, acknowledge the terrible effects of the assimilation policies and the pain experienced by Indigenous Peoples, and ask for pardon. Furthermore, Pope Francis has urged: "Never again can the Christian community allow itself to be infected by the idea that one culture is superior to others, or that it is legitimate to employ ways of coercing others."

7. In no uncertain terms, the Church's magisterium upholds the respect due to every human being. The Catholic Church therefore repudiates

those concepts that fail to recognize the inherent human rights of Indigenous Peoples, including what has become known as the legal and political "doctrine of discovery."

8. Numerous and repeated statements by the Church and the Popes uphold the rights of Indigenous Peoples. For example, in the 1537 bull *Sublimis Deus*, Pope Paul III wrote, "We define and declare ... that ... Indians and all other people who may later be discovered by Christians, are by no means to be deprived of their liberty or the possession of their property, even though they be outside the Christian faith; and that they may and should, freely and legitimately, enjoy their liberty and possession of their property; nor should they be in any way enslaved; should the contrary happen, it shall be null and have no effect."

9. More recently, the Church's solidarity with Indigenous Peoples has given rise to the Holy See's strong support for the principles contained in the United Nations Declaration on the Rights of Indigenous Peoples. The implementation of those principles would improve the living conditions and help protect the rights of Indigenous Peoples as well as facilitate their development in a way that respects their identity, language, and culture.

USCCB Statement on the "Doctrine of Discovery" (March 30, 2023)

WASHINGTON — The Dicasteries for Culture and Education and for Promoting Integral Human Development released today a Joint Statement on the "Doctrine of Discovery." The matter at issue involves documents (papal bulls) issued in the fifteenth century with regard to European exploration of land beyond continental Europe. Archbishop Paul S. Coakley of Oklahoma City and secretary for the U.S. Conference of Catholic Bishops (USCCB) has issued a statement in response to today's Joint Statement by the dicasteries:

> We are grateful to the Dicasteries for Culture and Education and for Promoting Integral Human Development for their Joint Statement on the "Doctrine of Discovery." The Joint Statement is yet another step in expressing concern and pastoral solicitude for Native and Indigenous Peoples who have experienced tremendous suffering because of the legacy of a colonizing mentality. We welcome the statement's renewed repudiation and condemnation of the violence and injustices committed against Native and Indigenous Peoples, as well as the Church's ongoing support for their dignity and human rights. In the centuries that followed the papal bulls at issue, many popes boldly proclaimed the God-given rights owed to all peoples, but we must also confront those moments when individual Christians lacked such boldness or clarity.
>
> As the Joint Statement points out, there were times when Christians, including ecclesiastical authorities, failed to fully oppose destructive and immoral actions of the competing colonial powers. In this regard, we, too, express deep sorrow and regret. In recent years here in the United States, dialogues among Catholic bishops and Tribal leaders have illuminated more aspects of this painful history, and, with humility, we wish to offer our continuing solidarity and support, as well as a further willingness to listen and learn. We will continue to support policies that protect the poor and vulnerable, and that will offer relief to Native

and Indigenous families who are struggling. Through Catholic charitable, health, and educational initiatives, we will continue to offer service to all people, with particular concern for those Native and Indigenous communities where the Church has been present. We support the ongoing efforts of various Catholic communities to make archival and historical records more easily accessible.

Finally, as the Joint Statement indicates, the centuries of history at issue are complex, and the term "doctrine of discovery" has taken on various legal and political interpretations that merit further historical study and understanding. The experiences and histories of different countries and different Native and Indigenous Peoples are distinct, and deserve further inquiry, although there are also opportunities for meaningful common understandings as well. As a Church, it is important for us to fully understand how our words have been used and misused to justify acts that would be abhorrent to Jesus Christ. We hope for more dialogue among Indigenous and Catholic scholars to promote greater and wider understanding of this difficult history. To that end, the USCCB and the Canadian Conference of Catholic Bishops are exploring how they may support an academic symposium. This initiative has also received encouragement from the Pontifical Committee for Historical Sciences, the Dicastery for Promoting Integral Human Development, and the Dicastery for Education and Culture.

May God bless with healing all those who continue to suffer the legacy of colonialism, and may we all offer true aid and support. By God's grace, may we never return to the way of colonization, but rather walk together in the way of peace.